The Story of

MARÍA ELENA

and KILTER's Jazz-Metal Opera

LA SUSPENDIDA

William Berger

The Prime Convergence Publications

New York

2023

The Prime Convergence Publications

New York, New York

Copyright © 2023

ISBN # 9798396037816

"Never be afraid of the dead… it's the living who'll fuck you over."

--My late mother, said frequently and often in Spanish

ACKNOWLEDGMENTS

In putting together this book, I primarily need to thank my husband Stephen J. Miller for his formatting and editorial prowess, and also for his support in every aspect of *La Suspendida*. For the whole experience of working on *La Suspendida*, I have many people to thank beyond my collaborators (who I name and discuss in this book). I need to mention the people at the venues where we've been workshopping this opera, especially New York's Nublu and Culture Lab LIC, and Montreal's Foufounes Electriques. I also want to express gratitude for the generosity and wisdom of my many friends in the New York music and theater community and especially for the encouraging words and enthusiastic support given by my comrades in the New York Heavy Music community.

Introduction

I was approached by Andromeda Anarchia and Laurent David to write the libretto for a jazz-metal opera they were thinking about based on the story of Carl Tanzler and his necrophiliac obsession with María Elena Milagro. A libretto (Italian for "little book") is the text, including lyrics and some amount of scene-setting, for an extended musical work such as an opera. I wrote a libretto for an opera called *La Suspendida* ("the Suspended Woman") and submitted it to them, revising it substantially as a work-in-process with them and Ed RosenBerg III, the saxophonist for David's band KILTER—and in fact am continuing to revise it even now. That libretto (as it stood at the time of publication) is included in this volume. A libretto has a backstory, a tale that can be told in prose, which is often (rather confusingly) called the "book" of an extended musical work. I began working on what I'll call the story of the opera before I wrote the libretto, of course, in order to roadmap the events of the work, some of which would then be elaborated as sung lyrics while others would be stage directions and narrative for instrumental passages. I continued to work on the story of the opera during and after submission of the libretto. That story is also included in this volume as "The Vaguely Haunting and Curiously Resonant Tale of María Elena, 'La Suspendida.'" Additionally, I wrote an essay about how this whole process came about and why I vibed with it so intensely. This essay is to be found in this book titled "Creating *La Suspendida*: a Memo from The Border." Laurent, Andromeda, and Ed each sent me short essays telling their experience of how they were drawn to this story and felt moved to write an opera about it. Those short essays are found in the chapter titled "Notes from the Creators." I also included bios of theirs and other collaborators on this project, the Growlers Choir and the string quartet SEVEN)SUNS, with information on where to find more of each of these remarkable artist's work. I am hoping that this collection of texts into the present book will interest you in pursuing my other writings and work, the music and creations of all of these remarkable artists, and above all, the extraordinary musical/theatrical journey that is the opera *La Suspendida*.

Table of Contents

Introduction..vii

The Vaguely Haunting and Curiously Resonant Tale of
María Elena, also known as "La Suspendida"................1

Notes from the Creators of *La Suspendida*...................41

    Intro to Notes..43

    Laurent David...45

    Andromeda Anarchia..................................49

    Ed RosenBerg III.......................................55

Creating *La Suspendida*: A Memo from The Border.......59

The Opera: *La Suspendida*......................................91

    Synopsis...93

    Libretto..95

The Collaborators of *La Suspendida,* bios and info.......123

About the Author..135

The Vaguely Haunting and Curiously Resonant Tale of

María Elena,

also known as

La Suspendida

It's really just like riding waves, she thought, as her body shook again.

It's just a matter of going with the rising and the falling rather than fighting against it... like ducks do... sometimes diving under the wave when its face is too threatening, sometimes floating over the crest with confident serenity, occasionally taking wing and flying over the tumult. Or not ducks, they're too funny. Swans. Yes, that's it... the way she imagined swans would ride the ocean waves, if a swan ever chose to (not that she had ever seen a swan on the beach or anywhere except in the placid fountains of the Parque Almendares): now dive under, now float over, now fly away. It's like a dance, really—and what *cubana* doesn't know how to dance almost as if by instinct?

And in how many other instances in life had she ridden the waves like a pro? It wasn't just swimming at the beach where she'd managed it, looking up at *las palmas* for orientation. It was in so many other situations in life. All of life, she considered, was riding waves. All energy is made of waves, as *este* Einstein had been saying for years. You could see it... feel it in everyday life: walking with elegance over the cobbled streets of Havana; swimming in Key West; giving birth; making love, or being made love to, or being used by men (whatever you want to call it). That, too, was best approached like riding a wave: sometimes moving away, sometimes bearing down, always dancing with and around the lumpish pounding of the men (which she knew only too well even now in her young years). And like that one time during her big journey across the Straits to Florida, when she and her mother boarded that creaky old steamer and for a little while thought they would perish at sea, tossed about the shoals just outside of the harbor of Key West. The steamer lurched several times, its planks creaking and its wrought iron supports clanging. Her mother's rigid spine fought the movement with determined willpower as she moved only to make the sign of the cross in these presumed final moments. But she turned away from her mother and saw the children of the voyage playing, as children will in any situation, making a great game out of falling and jumping up with the tossed vessel. And just as her mother was about to yell at the children to behave while she was having *los nervios*, the entire company was surprised... astonished... almost suspended between nervous breaths to realize there were no more waves, no more lurches of the ship or crashes of the sea against the hull. Everyone looked around nervously, smiling shyly at the serenity, hardly daring to believe the threat had passed. She stood and walked outside with no threat whatsoever, looking over the placid waters of the little harbor, as bright and smooth as the flat tip of an unrolled bolt of silk, to the waterfront taverns and quaint little hotels of her new home.

*

María Elena Milagro de Hoyos (also known by many variations of that name) was born in Cuba in 1909. Her father Francisco Hoyos was a cigar maker who set up a shop in Key West, Florida. Her mother was Aurora Milagro. In 1926, María Elena, already a celebrated beauty, married Luís Mesa, who was one year older than her. When María Elena suffered a miscarriage directly after the marriage, Luís left her and lived with his relatives in Miami. María Elena lived from then on with her parents in Key West.

*

Yes, she reminisced as she floated in the air above the foggy serenity, *pobrecito* Luís was scared by my viscera. He saw in it only death, as others later saw in my dead womb only life. How men have tried to make sense of me, and define me... and how poorly they've done it! My father playing with his little cigars, all those signs of symbols of *mi patria*, Cuba... Were they ever mine? I claim all my names, though, and all their rich meanings and allusions. Like so many Latins, I am rich in nothing except beautiful names. I am María, the humble handmaiden who is also the Queen of the Universe. And Elena, Helen, daughter of Zeus, wife of a worthless king, lover of a worthless handsome prince... so beautiful that the whole world fought a war for her, and the great city of Troy forgave her though her beauty meant its destruction. And

Milagros, of course, because miracles reverse the natural order. And Hoyos because I am a pit, a hole, where dreams of progeny and immortality go to die. And a *milagro de hoyos* because my holes are miracles too, not subject to the laws of physics.

"*Ven, hija,*" her mother said, fussing with their bags, bidding her daughter follow her ashore. But María Elena hadn't understood why she couldn't stay right where she was, on the boat, looking at the little ripples in the water, swaying back and forth, forever suspended between realms.

*

María Elena was stricken with tuberculosis, an incurable condition at that time. It was also a disease that had massive cultural implications about it, a certain mystique, it could even be said. The 19th Century had abounded in artistic souls afflicted with the disease, and the association between tuberculosis and the artistic temperament became axiomatic. The poet John Keats died of it at 25, and his fellow Romantic and friend Percy Bysshe Shelley suffered from it and would have died of it too had he not first died in a boat accident at 29. Edgar Allen Poe watched his young wife die of it, descending into madness and alcoholism (and moved to write "The Raven") through his vigil. The association of the disease with alluring women was particularly prevalent at this time: the pallor and wasting syndrome were found to amplify contemporary notions of feminine beauty and appeal (as, indeed, they still are among certain microcultures ["Goth," "heroin-chic" models, and so forth]). The celebrity Parisian courtesan Marie DuPlessis died of it at 23, inspiring her sometime-admirer Alexandre Dumas *fils* to write a revisionist novel and a very successful play about their affair (*La Dame aux caméllias*). The play became the basis for Verdi's subtly revolutionary opera *La traviata*, and later the blockbuster film *Camille* starring the face of the century, Greta Garbo. Tuberculosis was also the sign and symbol of *La traviata*'s spiritual daughter Mimì in Puccini's iconic opera *La bohème*, who has become the archetype of the inspiration of the artist's lifestyle. The macabre mystique did not pass away with the 19th Century and Romanticism: such 20th century prose giants as Anton Chekhov, Katherine Mansfield, and Franz Kafka died of it, and Nobelist Thomas Mann's 1924 novel *The Magic Mountain* is a study of people dying of it. The disease was thought to confer not only a macabre physical beauty on its victims, but also, with its fevers and aura of doom, a heightened sensitivity and acuity—in short, artistry.

*

Yes, thought María Elena as she remembered the morning she arrived in Key West—so like this present moment, and yet not—this now was a bit like the calm after that storm, the safe arrival in the harbor. The throes decreased, leaving nothing but rather delightful shivers in her thin but still beautiful body. There was a sort of city ahead of her, behind a stone wall like those pictures of ancient places like Jericho and Troy that looked so "forever" but were forever tumbling down. And there was a rather annoying light behind her, harsh, like Havana in June. But right where she stood, there was nothing but lovely silver blobs of cloudy gray paisley shapes, inciting and inviting

her to dance among them. Her long, loosened black hair swirled among the cloud-forms and her arms rose up in great arcs. She felt soft moisture caress her face and tingling everywhere, realizing that the rocking motion had begun again. It wasn't threatening now. It was perfectly marvelous. She was in charge of it somehow, as one can sometimes change directions in a dream, or even choose to fly in them. When the waves grew to the point of feeling almost dangerous, she felt a wonderfully refreshing pulse infused into her womb, causing her to dance in greater leaps and circles amid the silver cells of fog.

"This feels like home, right here," she said, to no one in particular. "…The first one I've ever known. It's neither Cuba nor Florida. It's neither hot nor cold. There is no weather at all, and I don't hate it. I can feel my body, yet I'm free from it." She laughed. "I never loved my body much anyway. It always felt like someone else. It's finally starting to feel right, right here, right now. *Curioso, no?* That feeling less can feel so right?" She turned back toward the ugly light. "*Adios, mundo viejo,*

marriage, home, family. *Adios, mamacita.* **But not** *adios* **to love, because there is love here, now, outside of time, in this place that is no place... better than any love I've known before. It feels good, it feels like nothing but pleasure. I reject the pain; I send it back home to the world of light where it belongs.** *¡Vaya, demonio!* **I choose the joy I just felt a moment ago, forever, here in this new land that's no land... this place with no weather."**
She danced on.

*

Carl Tanzler (he used many variations of this name) was born in the culture-rich city of Dresden in the Kingdom of Saxony, part of the German Empire, in 1877. He was a man of varied interests and insatiable scientific curiosity. His plans to explore the South Pacific were interrupted by the First World War. He was held in Australia, along with other enemy aliens, in an internment facility for the duration of the war. After the peace of 1918, Tanzler was sent to a prisoner exchange facility in neutral Holland and returned to

Germany. He found his mother safe and well after the upheaval, but his nation was, of course, in tatters. He married there and had two daughters. In 1926, he traveled to see his sister in Zephyrilis, Florida, soon joined by his wife and daughters. However, he left them all to take a job as a radiology technician in Key West.

It was at the Marine Hospital there in Key West that Tanzler first met the tuberculosis patient María Elena Milagro de Hoyos in 1930. He fell in love with her, feeling that she was the ideal woman that had been promised to him in a vision years before. (We have no evidence that María Elena either returned his feelings, nor had any particular feelings toward him whatsoever.) He took it upon himself to treat her case himself, although he was not technically a doctor, and offered her a series of alternative treatments. His prescriptions for her were no more effective than the doctors' were, although they were probably no worse either. The plain fact was that neither mainstream nor alternative science were of any effective use against tuberculosis at this time, and nothing known then could have prevented her death, which occurred on October 25th, 1931.

*

Other forms appeared as María Elena danced, silent in the dim distance, floating randomly but heading in the general direction of the stone wall. As if in response, still other forms appeared on the parapets of the Dead City and spoke in some strange yet now vaguely comprehensible language.

"Morning comes to the eastern shore of the western hemisphere," they muttered from the parapets, "revealing the shadows of those who died in continents' night. The newly dead of the Americas have gathered there across the sands, awaiting the summons we now proclaim. Arise, Shades! Fall in line for the grim parade, like single tears aggrandizing the ocean of perpetual death. Obey our command! We have forgotten time and light, as you must now forget as well. Come. We will teach you the timeless ways of this land."

Their voice-like emanations pulsed in rhythm as they announced the roll call of half the world's newly deceased, with their earthly addresses, ages, and causes of death.

"Kiko da Silva, Rio de Janeiro, Brazil... 17, knifed.

"Hattie Mae Johnson, Norfolk, Virginia... 89, loneliness.

"Ryan O'Malley, New York... 46, heart attack in office.

"Kwe'tshito of Kanahwahkee, Quebec... 52, homeless and frozen.

"Come, shed your names,
Your clocks, your pain...

"María Elena Milagros, Key West, Florida... 21, tuberculosis."

Their voices echoed, and then silence.

"María Elena Milagros, Key West, Florida... 21, tuberculosis..." they repeated. Then they

thundered, "All shades must comply! Attendance is compulsory!"

But María Elena did not comply. She remained dancing in her spot outside the walls of the Gates of Death, much to the annoyance of all the dead.

*

Tanzler paid for María Elena's funeral and had a mausoleum constructed for her corpse in Key West Cemetery. He visited the mausoleum almost every night for over a year, singing to her. He later claimed that her corpse would tell him—command him—to take her away from the grave. He obeyed the command in 1933. He removed the corpse and carted it home in a toy wagon, reassembling the crumbling bones with wire and creating a wig for her out of hair he had obtained from her mother Aurora under circumstances which have not been disclosed to history. He created a new skin for her out of silk, wax, and plaster, and stuffed her abdominal cavities with disinfectant-soaked rags to keep her form. Dressing her in lovely outfits, including stockings, jewelry, and gloves, he installed her in his bed and made love to her repeatedly as his wife.

*

Realizing the shadows of the dead would never shut up simply by being ignored, María Elena turned to address them, a beam of light from the upper world falling on her like a diva in a follow-spot.

"*Damas y caballeros*, distinguished colleagues of the dead, I thank you for your kind invitation to your world. I hate to be rude, but I fear I must decline your summons. I have the ability to do something rather novel: that is, remain here, in this place, eternally. I am not asking—as I'm sure so many do—to return to the Upper World. I have no interest in going back there. Cuba was no more a welcoming home for me than Key West, and my husband left me when I miscarried our child... You simply can't imagine I spent a spent a moment begging him to return or take me back, can you?" She laughed. "So you see I learned to seek out a home of my own that was neither on one side nor

the other, neither that country nor the other, depending on the kindness of neither one man nor the other. I may not have lived long, but I learned a thing or two in that short time. And when I fell sick, Tanzler prodded me with needles and devices… since men know how to do very little with women except poke them with one prong or another. But since my body lost its, shall we say, natural elasticity," she laughed again, "I have learned to use that man's continued prodding not to weaken me but to give me power, the power to choose my own home… the power to stay here, suspended between worlds."

The shades moaned and howled, whether in anger, astonishment, or sheer disbelief she could not tell. She flipped a long lock of her hair.

"You see I do not deceive you. I even get help from my mother, Aurora *la bella*. I think she was not prepared to let go of me either."

The death howls rose in volume. María Elena sighed.

"I have not been clear enough for your shadowy forms to comprehend, and I ask your forgiveness. Allow me to restate: *Aqui estoy*—here, in this place between your world and theirs… in this place…." She inhaled deeply and ran her hands down her face. "How curious, to have no weather! I rather like that. It suits me. And as long as that creepy little doctor keeps infusing my dusty pussy with the seminal life juice that re-creates on Earth, I cannot be fully dead, don't you see? Oh, I understand it is quite novel and untraditional. I will admit that this pervert and I are not your typical couple—not even your typical kinky couple. Yet it is, in spite of all expectation, working, and it is harming no one. Therefore, I declare that all may say this or that, but as for me…" she repeated the words as if the uttering of them tasted good, "as for me, I choose to remain here, suspended, in this place with no weather."

*

Tanzler kept María Elena's body in his—their—bed, but not exclusively. Witnesses many years later said they'd seen him through his living room window, dancing with her corpse to the most romantic Spanish-language songs of the day. And he replaced the fake skin and disinfecting stuffing as often as necessary, also giving her glass eyes so she could see the beautiful life he'd made for them.

*

"You cannot choose where to spend eternity," said the shadows. "That choice is made by immutable forces stronger than you."

"Oh, I make the choice for my own destiny," she replied casually, "but I have supernatural forces of my own helping me maintain it, don't I? I mean, first of all, there's this crazy man who's in love with me." She raised her fingers to her lips in anticipation of saying something very naughty, just as she used to do with her sisters when they talked about boys. **"If he's able to make love to me across dimensions of time and space and life and death, one might even say he's the best-hung man in the world! Of course, all men think they are**

extraordinary down there, don't they? But even you must admit this man, for all his other shortcomings, has a good claim on the honor of *la verga más increíble del mundo*. And imagine, it's all for me, at my disposal!"

A communal shudder erupted from the shadows.

"Please don't be angry at him. It's really not his choice. He, too, obeys supernatural forces. He is a slave of the Goddess of Love."

"There are no goddesses of love," said the shadows. "Venus and Ishtar and all of them are mere expressions of human psychology. And it is not these imaginary goddesses, but only the universal human fear of us, the Dead, that makes humans act like freaks."

"Then you're saying he is compelled to fuck a corpse—my corpse—because he has the same fear of death that everyone else has? Well, this is certainly an odd way to show such revulsion! But I don't care that you don't understand. I'm sure you're not the only ones. But understand this: I do not have to be dragged through your gates. Think of my still-vibrant earthly connection as a phallic 'green card' that gives me the right to live or die where I wish."

"No," cried the choir of the Dead. "If love is a god, as you insist, then so is time—one with the power to push you and all things in this direction."

"You don't know shit if you think Time is a stronger god than Love. How many lovers have loved beyond death? Didn't Thelma and Louise love into the abyss? Didn't Tristan and Isolde literally grow trees out of their graves and cause the trees' branches to intertwine? Do you even read?"

"Those lovers died together. They were equals. Their love did not inhabit separate worlds."

"But others did, and you allowed it!" she spat back. "Queen Victoria shaved Prince Albert's statue every day after he died. And Shah Jahan's wife lay buried in the world's finest monument. Even today people travel from all over the world to Agra to gaze upon it and swoon over how much he loved

> her in death. What is the Taj Mahal but pornography in marble?"

"They loved with their souls, not with their flesh—much less did they mingle living flesh with dead dust."

"I see no difference between loving with the soul and loving with the flesh, and neither do you. You don't even remember what flesh is. I do, because I still feel it in me. It is only the soul that sins. Flesh is pure and innocent, even when it is decayed."

> "It cannot be," insisted the Dead. "It will not pass the test of science or morals."

"Well you needn't take my word for it. Why don't you ask his grandmother, the Old Countess? She's back there, in your city somewhere." She laughed cruelly. "Oh, can't you find her? You can't tell one from another over there? At night all cats are gray? No matter. I'll tell you all you need to know." And she did.

*

Anna Constantia von Brockdorff was born in the Holstein province of Germany in 1680 to a family of the knight, or gentry, class. She was a bright girl, highly educated, rambunctious, and known as a troublemaker—all character assets she would retain for her long life. She was sent as a lady-in-waiting to the daughter of the local Duke of Schleswig, got pregnant in one castle or other (the fate of the child is unknown), returned to her parents, and took up with, eventually married, and secretly divorced a certain Baron Hoym. Presumed to be a noblewoman, she then showed up at the royal court of Dresden, where King Augustus of Poland and Saxony immediately fell in love with her and made her the official royal mistress. He gave her a title, Imperial Countess (*Reichgräfin*) of Cosel, and she gave him three children. She was, however, too vivacious—and far too meddlesome in the labyrinthine politics of court—to last long. She was replaced in the king's affections by a rival, a Polish countess, and was banished from court. After some intrigues in Berlin attempting to recover her former position, she was exiled to the foreboding and charmless castle at

Stolpen, at the very edge of Saxony—and she stayed in the castle for the remaining 49 years of her curious life.

The Countess of Cosel eventually accepted her fate. It is said that when she was offered her freedom years later, she declined it, informing the new king that her destiny was within the walls of Schloss Stolpen. She also became a great favorite of the local populace, and in turn she saw herself as the protectress of the people. Legends grew around her, but no one had anything in particular to accuse her of beyond being intelligent and high-spirited, even in captivity. She died in 1765 and was buried, appropriately enough, within the castle. Her grave can be visited there today.

Carl Tanzler was born in Dresden in 1877. He was convinced that Anna von Cosel was his ancestress, presumably by the king or perhaps one of her several other liaisons prior to her royal dalliance. He never specified. But he did use her name, along with others. While on his 1920 German certificate of marriage to Doris Schäfer, he signed himself simply Georg Karl Tanzler, his United States citizenship papers bore the name Carl Tanzler von Cosel. He was known to rather grandly sign some of his hospital records (in Key West, no less) as Count Carl Tanzler von Cosel.

*

"He said the old Countess was his grandmother," María Elena said, "but I doubt that. She lived 7 generations before him. And besides, all mortals think they're nobility, don't they? It's human nature. But whatever facts don't add up, the fact remains that she was real to him. He told me about her visitation many times, and how the air in the room changed when she was there, and how he could even smell her perfume. And what she told him was quite unforgettable.

'I am sent to you' she said, 'by the Goddess of Love Herself. By whatever name you know Her, Ishtar, Venus, Freia, or Rati, or a thousand others. Or you may not believe She exists at all, but all will obey Her, always. And whenever I speak for Her, all will obey me as well. I am Her slave as you, Sir, are mine. You may think She's a whore, but no matter. She's been called worse, and in fact She is worse.

She is also a thief, in that She makes people desire that which is not theirs to possess, and She is a demon in that She makes them want things that they know perfectly well will only bring them grief. The Emperor Caligula fucked his grandmother, and the Emperor Xerxes fell in lust with a tree, and the Princess Pasiphäe could only be satisfied by a bull—and those are merely the most notorious examples from classical antiquity. So it doesn't matter whether you like Her, or honor Her, or even believe in Her... you will do Her bidding, whoever you are.'

The Countess went on: 'Now I bring you a gift from Her, a new gift that has never been given to a mortal before, and even more outlandish than a desire for a bull, or a tree, or even an old relative like me. Are you not delighted by this favor? Don't you feel special to be given the order to commit an absolutely original sin? Because, you see, you will love a woman who doesn't even exist yet, the subject of a mistress who is yet to be. We've probed your mind and other receptacles of desire, and we will create her to come to you in the future.

And you may love her, and take her flesh forever, and evermore after that, until...'" María Elena trailed off, as if she had lost her narrative thread. "And this," she told the shadows, "is exactly what came to pass for poor old Tanzler. Isn't it delicious?" she said, dancing again and seeming refreshed and renewed in her energy.

The shadows bellowed "If love and sex are the same, then your man Tanzler sins twice against the God of Time, since as you say, he fucked you both before birth and after death!"

She sneered. "Didn't my husband Luís do the same when he left me because I miscarried, bearing a corpse? All he saw in our stillborn child was the death of his own future, he saw his own failure— just the first of many." She shook her long, waxen hair. "Everybody does this, don't you see? Everyone is a necrophiliac, buying time in the next world with wages from the past world. Every time they buy a stock, or plant a tree, it's the same as fucking the future. To find a way around death is the categorical imperative of love. It's what love is.

Time has nothing to say about it. If it is love, it lasts, or else it is false, and time may have its way with it."

"Fucking a corpse is a sin – against Nature, against Time, and against Love!" cried the shadows.

"Oh, you self-righteous prigs!" she snarled. "Everyone fucks the dead! They're no better than him and me. They're just less forthright. You don't believe me? Tell me again how much you love Princess Diana and cherish her memory. And poor, dear Marilyn Monroe and all the 'celluloid heroes who never really die,' and the 'diva,' la divina Callas! Why can't you or anyone on earth let them rest? And wait…" She squinted through the limbic miasma. "What's that I see over there, suspended like me? Isn't that the body of Lenin, embalmed but unburied, visited even now by his few remaining devotees? And let's not even talk about Jesus Christ, you perverted hypocrites! He for Whom you get on your knees and Whose body you ingest, and Whom you beg to come, and then to come again."

"Your sin is greater than the worshipers of the dead because you upend all that is and all that will be. You are not original. You are merely desperate to cling to life—and you imagine we haven't seen that before! You are clinging by the smallest phallic thread, the dick of Damocles. Let go! Let go…"

"It's only a sin this time because it is a woman who commits it. That's when people start speaking about sin and perversion and crimes against nature. So I see that even the Dead are no better than all those hypocrites up there in the world of the Light. But I'll show you your own shame," she said to them, finding a new power in her own voice. "I'll show you how much power I have and I'll make you watch me in action so you'll not be able to deny your own hypocrisy. Your hatred for me inspires me to new expressions of love. I've never felt stronger," she felt her own breasts, "and I've never felt sexier than I do now. I declare my body to be my own, at last. And this body will command any who come to it, and behold how I will be obeyed!"

*

Florinda Milagro, María Elena's sister, heard rumors of Tanzler living with the corpse. She confronted Tanzler one night in 1940, nine years after María Elena's death, and the body was discovered in his house. Tanzler was arrested for grave robbing but not for necrophilia—there was no evidence of necrophilia submitted at the trial and no mention was made of any tampering with the corpse's vagina until several years later. It would have been difficult to indict Tanzler for necrophilia anyway since no one had thought to make applicable laws against it (the laws have since been articulated and refined, largely because of this case). Even the grave robbing charges were inapplicable because the statute of limitations had passed. The case was widely reported in the press, and the public—who had been fed tales of Tanzler dancing with the corpse in his home, but only heard of necrophilia by innuendo—grew to think of Tanzler as a benighted but harmless romantic. He was released and reunited with his wife and family in mainland Florida. María Elena's body was buried in an unmarked grave to prevent further tampering.

*

María Elena twirled in the air and dissipated the silver clouds of the foyer of death, and the naked body of a living man crawled toward her.

"Vile!" the Dead cried as one. "Vile! He reeks of flesh! We never thought we'd have to tolerate such foulness again, yet you bring him before us?"

She straddled over him and declaimed, "Obey me, thrall! Make love to me again on my order, but harder! I will hold nothing back this time, and neither will you. And the Dead will have to watch it all!" She rose up and down on his helpless form, growing stronger which each thrust she commanded from him. "Harder! Harder, you slave! The more I grind down on your cock, the stronger I become. Give it all to me, even your life itself if I so demand it. My corpse is your dungeon, drone. Tell me what a favor I'm doing you by letting your living member in my inner dead womb. My corpse, your

dungeon… isn't that so? Right? Tell me, you dumb piece of meat! I can't believe I even need this from such a lowdown servant, but it is my triumph—my second triumph! You fell in love with me, and now I will make you prove it, in front of everyone living and dead. Give me the seed that waters my dusty Alpha hole. Admit how you love it, scumbag. You're nothing without me. Nothing! You'd be forgotten, annihilated by history and legend if it weren't for me and my sacred temple of dead cunt. This is how much you're my slave. My corpse… your dungeon… but at least you're still alive, between my legs and between the pages of history. Now give me everything you've got, you filthy freak—and shoot it in me so hard that I blast off to the next dimension!"

*

Although Tanzler reconciled with his wife Doris, and María Elena's body was buried at last, neither his obsession nor María Elena's journey were quite finished yet. Rumors and pulp journalism persisted and persist still. Tanzler is known to have created a death mask of María Elena and an effigy of her body attached to it, which he continued to live with (and sleep with). He was found lying next to it when his body was discovered three days after his own death in 1952 at the age of 75. Many maintained that this was actually the original corpse which he had contrived to retrieve somehow. Others said they had proof that he had actually poisoned her when he was treating her, and he had planned all along to love her as a corpse. The facts are unknowable *qua* facts. They became history, then journalism, then legend, then art (several songs, ranging from alt-indie to death metal, have been written about Tanzler), and most prodigiously as fill for cable television documentary. Each iteration of the story has modified, morphed, or warped it according to the needs of the moment, but its core persists. The public taste for the distasteful tale has not diminished with the passage of time.

*

María Elena felt herself charged up, as much by her own voice and words as by anything being done to

her from outside her body. As her energy level grew, she heard the voices of the Dead crescendo as well, until the sound reached what seemed like a point of explosion. Tanzler's writhing body flailed more wildly with her brightening aura and their swell of sound until he, too, seemed to shatter into tiny fragments like stars shooting out of a quasar, a pulverized cloud of dying light. The silver clouds crept back like a fog, as quiet settled again on the plains before the Gates of Death.

"Where am I now?" she wondered. "I haven't moved, but this whole realm has moved under me. How can this be? What does it mean?"

The silence gave way to a pulsing chorus from the parapets of the Dead City's walls. "Morning comes to the eastern shore of the western hemisphere, revealing the shadows of those who died in continents' night. The newly dead of the Americas have gathered there across the sands, awaiting the summons we now proclaim."

"This, again?" she thought. "Do I have to hear this stupid song again?" She covered her ears. "I need to block them out. I wish I had music to drown out their droning." She tried to sing, but no sound came from her. Instead, she heard their chorus continue, as she had heard them before...

"Arise, Shades! Fall in line for the grim parade, like single tears aggrandizing the ocean of perpetual death. Obey our command!"

She had an idea: "I wish I could fuck the sound away, fuck even louder and more dominant than last time, and not have to hear the choir of the Dead."

"We have forgotten time and light, as you must now forget as well. Come. We will teach you the timeless ways of this land."

They resumed their roll call of the recently dead – new names, but the song remained the same as before:

"Elgin McKay, Kingston, 24... gunshot.

"Catalina Pérez, Veracruz, 16... died in childbirth.

"Leonie Laroche, Tadoussac, 91... fatigue.

"Dave Martin, Provincetown, 36... overdose."

"*¡Ay, chingada!*" she uttered. "This annoys the crap out of me. Tanzler, come! Serve me again, as hard and as well as last time. Fill my dark, dank womb again on my command with your seed from the world of light, so I may stay suspended between the two realms."

The roll call resumed:

"Raúl Rossi, La Plata, 47... cancer.

"Ana Fernandes, Bahia, 51... cause unknown.

"Suzy Kowolski, Asbury Park, 56... car crash.

"Carl Tanzler, Key West, 75..."

"Tanzler?" María Elena jumped hearing the name. "Dead? Tanzler is dead? How can this be? How can he serve me now? How can anyone? Is there anyone else like him who'd answer the call to serve a body like this? Oh, men! You're all quitters! You all deceived me! I couldn't depend on any of you there, and not one of you can fix me here. How can you die on me?"

The chorus explained: "Tanzler, sometimes called Doctor, sometimes called Count, Herr von Tanzler—cause of death: heart attack… during sex with a corpse."

She stood motionless for a moment, stunned, and then laughed the bitter laugh of the newly wise. "So, that's how it ends? He put his best part into the void, and the void sucked his whole being through to the other side. What an epic orgasm—so intense he had to die for it. And it's the last irony, the last cruel joke to cap off the harsh lessons of both of my lives."

The choir chanted louder, but without words. She screamed. "No! I don't want to die again yet. I died once—too soon. I don't want to do what's expected of me now, be part of a faceless crowd, lose my own voice among theirs. Let no borders hold me in! Let me fly above them! I've done it before… why not now? I am unique, created by supernatural powers to exist before birth and persist after death. I am La Suspendida, the Genre of One!"

Choral words became discernible: "María Elena Milagros de Hoyos, 43... Key West."

She nodded her head in grudging assent. "Ahhh, it's not going to go away this time, is it?" They continued: "Cause of death: cessation of life support. Original death, age 21... Tuberculosis."

She drew a deep breath of the murky air of Limbo.

"So be it. *Adios*, lover, and body of mine, and songs, and memories. No more messages to or from the living world, no more need to pretend to be alive, no more need to pretend at all, to float..."

She discerned words in the voices of the dead – not new words, but ones she hadn't been able to make out before.

"Come, daughter. Come home. *Ven, hija*."

She shook her head, walking in a little circle. "I thought I cheated both life and death, finding myself ruling in my own realm between two massive kingdoms." She clucked her tongue. "It was a dream, an illusion. It still meant depending on someone else to keep me hanging there—a perv, a freak, but a man all the same, like the others. I didn't want to need him. I didn't want to whore my corpse to him or anyone. But when I tried to show control, it was too much for the laws of physics. My brief stint as a Dominatrix was so awesome that it blasted a hole through time and space, and I flew through it to another dimension. Yet it wasn't all a fake, was it?" She felt herself standing tall. "It wasn't all for nothing. It doesn't feel like it was. That blast through the membranes of space beyond time, that was... enjoyable, satisfying. What was it that I unleashed?" She touched herself between her legs and brought her fingers to her own lips. "I wonder. Was that... love?"

The chorus resumed: "Come with us. It's ok to join a choir once you've sung your solo. Come with us. This is the home you've always sought."

"Yes," she said. "It's my true mother that's calling me home. Not the old Countess, or even my mother Aurora—but the earth, cradle of all. How is it I never realized how much I craved this home, through both my lives and two halves of death? I just didn't know how to go home as a victor, not a victim. But I see it's not so hard after all."

"Come with us. It's ok to join a choir once you've sung your solo. It's not like it was before. It's ok to die now."

"Yes," she said. "Let's go home at last. I'm tired and ready to rest. Yes."

*

NOTES FROM THE CREATORS OF

LA SUSPENDIDA

Introduction to

Notes From the Creators of *La Suspendida*

The score of *La Suspendida* was created by KILTER in collaboration with Andromeda Anarchia, with contributions from other musical partners including The Growlers Choir and Seven)Suns. Here is some background commentary from Laurent David of KILTER, Andromeda, and Ed RosenBerg III of KILTER.

La Suspendida: An Opera of Life, Death, and Beyond
by Laurent David

As a composer and producer of the experimental opera *La Suspendida*, I am proud to share the creative journey that brought this unique production to life. *La Suspendida* is a monodrama that explores the liminal space between life and death, where the protagonist, María Elena Milagros, finds herself suspended after passing away. The opera features a combination of jazz, new music, metal, and contemporary music, and it tells the story of María Elena's quest for self-discovery and empowerment through a series of encounters with the dead.

To bring this project to fruition, I collaborated with a talented group of musicians and artists, including Andromeda Anarchia, the string quartet SEVEN)SUNS, the Growlers Choir, and my own jazz-metal trio KILTER, as well as the librettist Will Berger. Each of these collaborators brought a unique set of skills and perspectives to the table, and together, we were able to create a musical and theatrical experience that is truly one-of-a-kind.

The musical style of *La Suspendida* draws from a range of influences, from the atonal melodies of new music to the aggressive rhythms of metal. Andromeda Anarchia, the singer who plays the role of María Elena Milagros, showcases her versatility as a vocalist by utilizing operatic singing techniques as well as screams and growls. Meanwhile, the Growlers Choir provides an eerie and unsettling backdrop with their guttural growls and whispers.

The narrative structure of *La Suspendida* is linear, with one exception in the form of a flashback. The story is told from the perspective of María Elena, who takes control of her life when she finds herself in *La Suspendida.* The music follows the narrative closely, with each composition and arrangement designed to evoke a specific mood and emotion in the audience. Visually and theatrically, *La Suspendida* is still in the development stage, but we envision a production that is immersive and engaging. In the concert format, María

Elena Milagros and the Choir of the Dead act out scenes to accompany the music. In the future, we hope to expand the production into a full-fledged opera with set designs and costumes that enhance the audience's experience of the story.

The collaboration process for *La Suspendida* was one of experimentation and exploration. Ed Rosenberg III, the bass saxophone player in KILTER, served as the composer/arranger and brought together the various sketches into a cohesive whole. Will Berger, the librettist, provided the lyrics and helped shape the story. Meanwhile, the performers themselves were involved in the creative process, with Andromeda Anarchia bringing her own ideas and interpretations to the character of María Elena.

In conclusion, *La Suspendida* is a unique and powerful work of experimental opera that pushes the boundaries of what is possible in terms of musical style and narrative structure. It is the result of a collaboration between a talented group of musicians and artists who each brought their own vision and expertise to the project. I am honored to have been a part of this project, and I look forward to seeing it continue to evolve and grow in the years to come.

A Note from Andromeda Anarchia

A few years ago, I happened to find a video of the Growler's Choir and was thrilled! What a great idea! I said to Laurent David, "Actually, there should be an opera—an opera with a Growler's Choir." Laurent David was then crazy enough to realize this idea, together with his metal-jazz trio KILTER.

I have had the great honor of singing/growling for KILTER several times. I have always been interested in anything that involves creative musical style crossovers and where I can use the voice as a versatile instrument. KILTER creates this kind of music. A music of the in-between. Somewhere between Metal and Jazz. But all three musicians have a classical music background too. This opens a lot of possibilities and crazy ideas. Like for example writing a jazz metal opera. An opera about a woman who is in the in-between.

To me, an opera is an ode to the human voice, a celebration. The voice as the centerpiece of musical and emotional expression… It's a larger-than-life experience. Big and thundering. With lightning flashing deep into our senses—waking us up, inspiring us. Opera moves us. Singing makes us feel alive, connects us. To me, the experience of hearing or performing an opera comes close to what I also feel from listening (and playing on) church organs.

A church organ is something truly great and impressive—like an opera, a huge sound, with pipes that can carry our melodies in all directions, far into the sky, through all atmospheres… right into the universe…. Well, that was my thought/imagination as a child. I gave my very first concert in front of an audience on a church organ. To this day I have a special love for this instrument. I loved playing with all those stops and sounds. I can mix the sound the way I feel the passage needs to be expressed. All the colors of the instrument, I can move them with my hands, gliding over the color palette like with a brush, coloring the composer's painting.

That's how I look at the voice, too. I don't want to use just one color (like for example the one of bel canto). I want to use the whole organ that is my voice and my body. Singing style-wise, I don't want to use just one way of singing, but all the ones I like.

KILTER has written a jazz metal opera, which requires a "voice organist" as a soloist.

Starting as a classical trained soprano (who grew up singing blues, rock and soul/r'n'b music), then with voice training excursions into the world of jazz and free-improvised as well as experimental music to my current singing home, extreme metal, this opera is a dream come true. What a challenge! As a musician... and especially as a singer.

This opera is the most difficult music I have ever sung. Not just from a singing or musical point of view… the subject is delicate and requires a lot of sensitivity. The role of María Elena must be interpreted with a lot of empathy, courageous expression, and most of all with dignity.

Vocally, it's like walking a tightrope—very demanding, sometimes it even feels a bit dangerous. But on an emotional level, the role of María Elena demands everything I've experienced in my life in terms of extremes to be able to portray it convincingly. A not easy self-confrontation! I first had to find the right color palette within myself to color the portrait of María Elena with my singing, according to KILTER's and William Berger's drawings. The opera is about a woman, María Elena, who existed. She was real, her story was real, her post-mortal fate was real, too—shocking, unbelievable, and surreal as it is to most of us. Yes, this role is extreme because her story was extreme. But this opera is not about sensationalism. This opera is about dignity.

William Berger and KILTER have created a unique crossover work that focuses on this very theme of dignity. An opera, huge just like an organ: it stirs souls, moves our hearts, it provokes thought, it triggers many conversations (among us musicians as well as the audience), it connects. The music connects the musicians with the audience, the story of María Elana with us, the hereafter with the here and now. A highly complex as well as morbid theme is made approachable, almost tangible, with a great sense of drama, aesthetics, and sensuality, despite its super-size. It's so moving and touching.

And like everything that is treated with dignity, it is beautiful.

A Note from Ed RosenBerg III

When I think about *La Suspendida*, I think about death: how we deal with death, and how we deal with the feeling that sometimes death is unfair. The story takes as its jumping off point the death of a young woman. The opera is about how everyone deals with it, including the young woman herself.

When a person dies too young, it feels profoundly unjust—like a theft. But there is no recourse with death. Nothing to say or do that can change the cold truth. And in that fog of mourning, we might consider any option, offer anything, make any deal, to undo what we know deep down cannot be undone.

This is where our story exists. Tanzler's inability to let go leads him to the unthinkable. He can't let go, almost literally. But María Elena can't let go either. She is holding on just like Tanzler. She's trying to find some control somewhere, somehow. I imagine her thinking "That was it? That was my life? It is not fair! I should be able to have the life I want!!!" María Elena, having just died, is profoundly disappointed. Out of that grows a rage-filled determination to define her own life (and death). She tries to stay connected to the living for as long as she can. In our mythic fantasy, she uses Tanzler's obsession (so to speak) to her advantage. But ultimately Tanzler's death reminds her of the inevitable, and she must accept her own death.

I remember an early meeting with Will where we arrived at the phrase, "It's okay to die." That's the lesson that we all must learn eventually, from both sides of the story. The person dying must let go, but so must the living.

While composing the opera, I tried to focus on the universality of both characters. We are all María Elena, scared of letting go and dying, wanting to pretend that we are in control and can decide how the story ends. But we are also Tanzler, holding onto those we've lost, reliving our grief over and over. María Elena raging against the choir of the dead is all of us. We don't want our stories to end.

While composing the final Lullaby of the opera, I was very focused on the final word, "Yes." This "yes" is María Elena's acceptance of her fate. Her peace with the life she had, and her welcoming of the coming mystery of non-existence. I can only hope that when my time comes, I can find the grace that María Elena has in her last moment. Yes.

CREATING *LA SUSPENDIDA:*

A Memo from "The Border"

Creating *La Suspendida*:
A Memo from "The Border"

This opera was born, appropriately enough, during a time of suspended activity: the COVID shutdown.

I'd been putting together showcases called "Mergers and Compositions" with the remarkable musician and person-who-makes-music-happen-in-others Nicholas Horner in his Brooklyn loft—all very casual goopings of works-in-progress and new collaborations, established artists and blushing art-virgins, music, spoken word, some dance and extemporaneous living visual art and quite a bit of "what even IS this?" served up with camaraderie and, when I could manage it, plates of homemade empanadas. When it was no longer possible to do these events live, we did a "Mergers On-Line." This gave us the advantage of showcasing work (videos mostly, perforce) from all over. Even Nick Horner himself had moved to Knoxville to begin new adventures in that world I'm told exists beyond New York and L.A.. Well, this one spoke to that one who spoke to the other one which led me to Andromeda Anarchia, hunkering out COVID in her sometime home of Paris. Everyone told me, "You of all people need to get to know Andromeda—she's another opera-metal person." (There aren't a lot of us who are Metalheads and opera fans at the same time, but we exist, and there are actually more of us than you'd expect.) For Andromeda, it was more than a matter of affinity for both genres. She had the almost unique ability to sing within the demanding strictures of both traditions: she could roll out bel canto roulades like a precision-obsessed Swiss conservatory student (which, in fact, was precisely what she once was), and she could honk out guttural growls like a Black Metal Bitch from literal Hell (which was also, in some sense, what she was). What impressed me even more was her facility in switching between these two vocal dimensions with a dexterity that left the ears with a wonderful case of aural whiplash. Her video with the equally genre-bending trio "Imperial Triumphant" was fascinating and perfectly delightful.

The connection was established. Within a week, Andromeda was sending notes saying she and a certain Laurent David wanted to Zoom-talk to me from Paris. Sure, why not. We Zoomed. Laurent was the bass-player/composer for the jazz/metal (more genre-bending!) trio KILTER, and he and she had ideas they wanted to run by me. There was this story from history—or some version of history—they were interested in… He told me the broad outlines of the story of Tanzler and María Elena, and sent me a few links for further (but not too detailed, yet) reading. They asked me what I thought. My first thought was that confessing this prurient interest in a story of extended necrophilia to a total stranger was fucking weird. And my second thought was that I wanted to hear more, which was even weirder. So we Zoomed again. What did I think? What even was this? Was it an opera? Why?

I told them it was definitely an opera, but only if it were told from María Elena's point of view, not Tanzler's. His point of view was a three-to-five minute song.

That's as much time as was needed to say, basically, "Oooh oooh oooh, I'm so weird and I screw a corpse and wow death is erotic, oooh oooh ooooh." And in fact I learned soon after that there were songs about Tanzler, including one by a band I admire greatly, The Black Dahlia Murder. I had even heard it ("Deathmask Divine," 2007) but had never thought to delve into the story or the lyrics beyond thinking, "Oooh oooh oooh yeah man, death and stuff...." Which is not to say it isn't an excellent song. It is. But it said everything it had to say about Tanzler the Necro. What, however, if we looked at the story from María Elena's point of view? And what if she weren't merely a (distinctly) passive victim, but had some agency in this course of events? In that case, we had an opera on our hands. I was thinking of *Madama Butterfly* as a model: she reads as a passive victim in the synopsis but is so much more interesting than that on the stage because the music clearly tells us she is the motivator of all events, including her own tragic destiny. When I thought about it, this held true for all the most interesting women in opera: Brünnhilde, Carmen, Norma, and Salome (a name that would come up repeatedly in this process). They all died in the end, but were the motivators, the characters who mattered. Because, (I said over the Zoom), the only reason to write an opera—and here I remember pausing at some length, Obama-like, for effect—was to give voice to characters who would not have sufficient voice in any other medium. In the dead María Elena, a defiled corpse asserting sexual dominance, I announced that we had discovered/would create the ultimate diva role.

Great, they said. Can you write the libretto? You betcha, I responded. And it was only later—and even as recently as reading Laurent's and Andromeda's and Ed's essays included in this book—that I realized they'd already decided all these things about María Elena on their own, and knew how this opera should be long before I came on board. In fact, these Zoom convos were less a chance for me to dazzle them with my aesthetic insights than a sort of job interview for librettist of the work whose exigencies they already knew. This is galling, of course, but it's also the way my best literature professors worked with me ages ago, letting me imagine I had arrived at Great General Truths by my own intellectual superpowers when they could have just as easily told me each of these things themselves in a single sentence. It was the sort of thing that led to me to such *apercus* as "Wait! You guys, I'm realizing now it's almost as if Ovid's narrative style reflects his subject matter, with one story seamlessly turning into another the way bodies turn into other things. OMG that's CRAZY!" While they no doubt thought, "Well DUH." But instead they said: "Very good, William."

There were several aspects of the story that reverberated for me specifically, however, and felt personal and independent of any reasons the others were drawn to this grisly tale. There was an immigration story here that struck me immediately. Both Tanzler and María Elena were immigrants and in fact refugees—he from World War I and she from… what? I don't know exactly, but Cubans don't leave for Florida (even back then) just because they think it will be prettier there. It isn't. It so happened that I was deep-diving into my own family history just at that time—or rather, looking into the murky history beyond the oft-repeated family legends. My father's family were Jews from… well, I wasn't exactly sure and am still learning, but they had some Eastern European roots. My father died when I was 11 and I got most of his and their story from others who provided me with a mix of hazy memories and self-glorifying mythology. In fact, I had recently gone to a military archive in Montreal to ask, in my bad French, about my paternal grandfather who, I had always heard, emigrated from Lithuania and served in the "Royal Canadian Fusiliers" in World War I. Well, there never was any such military unit as the Royal Canadian Fusiliers but there was a Mount Royal Fusiliers, so off I went to their armory. The archivist there asked my grandfather's name. "Je ne sais pas," I managed. It was William Berger when he died in 1931 in New York at the unfortunate age of 31, so his Staten Island tombstone says, but I had no clue what it had been in his Canadian phase. Well, was he Anglophone or Francophone? "Je ne sais pas," I repeated, although knowing what little I know about that side of the family, he was assuredly Whatever-was-needed-in-the-moment-phone, like the character from *Candide* who is "so easily assimilated," and whose "father spoke a high-middle Polish" but after half an hour in Buenos Aires is speaking "Spanish" (*"¡Por favor! ¡Toréador!"*) and dancing a tango. And so forth.... (Thanks to the patient ministrations of said archivist, I did find out more about this mysterious individual after whom I was, *mutatis mutandis*, named; although, I didn't learn much about him, and the process continues today.)

My mother's family from Mexico is much better attested in history, thanks in large part to the bureaucratic obsessiveness of the Spanish Empire and the all-but-compulsory baptismal records dating back to the Conquista in Mexico itself and back to the Second Crusade—no lie—in *la madre patria* (Spain). This millennial memory, however, is no better guarantor of exactitude than the Jewish family's mistiness. *Au contraire*. Legend and myth trump facts even when the facts are well documented. Story takes precedence over history. Take my great-grandmother for instance, who I knew well and who lived with us when I was growing up. She fled the Mexican Revolution to this country (to New York City, unlike most other refugees who went to the American southwest—but that's a whole other *megillah*) in 1916, harboring no nostalgia whatsoever for the old country. And why should she? She had two brothers (both priests)—and two sisters (both whores)—all four of whom were killed (shot, specifically) in the Revolution. So much for *México querido y lindo*. Yet, her distaste for the old country notwithstanding, she never learned one word of English despite living in the United States until her death in 1978. She cooked the ancient recipes but retained no affection for the tedious and labor-intensive traditional methods—she thought frozen food and pre-packaged tortillas were simply marvelous. I've never found out if her story about her siblings was true in the sense of having actually happened, and I can't commit the time and diligence it would take to suss out the cold facts. But it always struck me as a quintessentially Mexican tale, encapsulating the national psyche and history in one single fold like a cosmic truth-taco. And perhaps that, rather than any Anglo-Saxon sense of factual accuracy, was the true point of the story. My great-grandmother's sense of authentic identity lay not in her citizenship or her clichés of being an old woman chopping food for hours and making tortillas by hand. It lay in her stories.

The Mexican side of the family (along with my Italian-born maternal grandmother) migrated from New York to L.A., as so many other Americans did after World War II, and so did the post-war remnants of my father's Jewish family. Being Jewish and Mexican is not so strange a thing there as it seems to be here (back in New York). There is a preponderance of Jews in Los Angeles, and there is a preponderance of Mexicans, and occasionally they interact, and people like me happen. Yet even there, back then, my existence seemed to annoy people on all sides of the equation with its uncategorizability. I was always an asterisked personage. When the conversation turned to, "What are you?" (This referring to ethnicity—a common topic in the Asian-majority town, Monterey Park, in Los Angeles County where I grew up from birth to age 14.) I would explain at length and sometimes be told, "Oh, so you're really nothing at all." They didn't mean to be as dismissive as that sounded to my impressionable ears. I came to understand that they meant I didn't fit into any of their extant categories. Still, it's a fucked-up thing to say to a kid, and my internal (usually) unspoken reaction was "fuck you, I'm everything!" I slowly began the process of understanding that my ethnic identity was "Mixed," and that Mixed is something authentic in itself. Mixed counts, and it beats the snot out of that charming box I always had to check off on forms, "Other." Furthermore, I came to realize that Mixed is the very essence of the American immigrant story—as was telling (and sometimes making up) stories. Immigrants don't want the border patrol agents or the exit control officers or the Cossacks or the Federales to know their business. Even after assimilating here to various degrees, a sense of reticence remains. It's a New York tenement cliché to shut the front door or close the curtains because "the landlord don't need to know my business." A propensity to guard the cold facts, even from one's own progeny—even including who they are—is another product of the immigrant experience.

All Americans are immigrants. Yes, all—even the indigenous nations. They, too, moved around the continent before the Euros showed up, and then a good deal more after. To say they are the exception to the immigrant designation is yet another dehumanization of the Native American story. And even if you are born in the United States, you will move within the United States, which is a key aspect of the American migration story. Just ask any black person in Chicago whose great-grandparents came from Mississippi—and you won't have to search far to find this person. Or ask anyone like me who's bounced between New York and L.A. their whole lives. And even if you live and die in the same spot where your family has lived for generations, you're still an immigrant because America will move under your stationary feet. Ask any middle-aged-or-older person whose roots run back several generations in the very spot where they still live, and they'll tell you that they can hardly recognize the place anymore. America has moved and made them migrants through the machinations of time, because time, too, is a form of immigration. America is not, and never has been, like Imperial China or Pharaonic Egypt, both said to have achieved static perfection like a ball that has rolled to the center of a bowl. Our greatness lies in our mutability. America is a Limbo through which you pass, even if you stand perfectly still, and you (no matter who or where you are) are a citizen of it.

People look to binaries to help guide them through a confusing world: you must be This, or else you are That. There is no Other. Except there is, and not just for Ol' Mixed-Up Me. It's also true in the politics of language. Los Angeles was always thought of as a functionally bilingual city, except it's much more polylingual than that. (Korean and Tagalog, anyone?) In the last few years, I've spent a growing amount of time in Montreal, the world's most notoriously bilingual city, and learned that it, too, is linguistically poly rather than bi. There are Asian languages making themselves heard, and Eastern European ones. Some of the many new Hispanic immigrants there are like my great-grandmother—they're simply never going to learn a language other than Spanish "not no way, not no how" because (I suspect) there is this deep-seated conviction that God speaks Spanish. (The Emperor Charles V, who spoke most every European language, thought so.) And which Spanish? That of Mexico? If so, which part? Or Puerto Rico, Cuba, the Dominican Republic, or any of the South American countries? The same holds true for the old binary standbys, French and English: which version? British, American, or Indian (as in South Asian) English? And don't even start thinking about which version of French (standard Parisian, proper *québécois*, Acadian, or urban slang *joual*) is to be emphasized and legally supported—your head will explode. Oh, right, then there are the Indian (as in Indigenous) languages. Don't imagine for a moment that there is any unity on this subject. Speakers of Mohawk and Innu-aimun, the two most widespread indigenous languages of Montreal, have no historical or linguistic *entente* for each other.

Binaries are inherently reductive, and to draw imaginary lines between simplified dualities is unsophisticated, uninstructive, and ultimately unhuman. Taken to extremes, drawing lines recalls the infant's need to delineate, define, and demand that which belongs to them. The Border Wall was much in the news during this time. That right-wing wet dream was obviously a psychological (as opposed to practical) response to the border crisis: an infantile need to build a monument to Delineation: "us HERE, them THERE, WHAAAAH!" The persistent anti-trans movement is the exact same thing. You must be This or That but cannot be any Other. I'm not trans, but I don't fit perfectly into any of the existing binary definitions meant to eradicate the possibility of trans… And neither do you, whoever you are. It is simply not possible to be all-male or all-female as the terms are understood by biology or sociology, so you can't be perfectly non-trans, either. We are all in this place between the poles of definition. They call it a border, as if it were a thin line, but it is actually the opposing poles, and not the so-called border, that are the narrow extremes.

By my mixed ethnicity, my flare for languages inherited from my "easily assimilated" forbearers (other than my resolutely monolingual great-grandmother), and my non-standard sexual identity (I'm cisgendered and even skew a little butch, but I'm authentically gay as fuck, if you couldn't tell already simply because *of course* the person writing this would be), I learned that The Border is not a thin line between states (of the world or of existence): The Border is a state of existence of its own. And it's a much larger country than it is usually imagined to be. Most of us live there most of our lives. As I wrote the opera's outline, *La Suspendida* became a Tale of The Border for me. And let me tell you something about immigrants detained at The Border: you're one of them. We all are.

COVID passed and semi-COVID followed.

Laurent and Andromeda returned to Brooklyn, where Ed RosenBerg III and Kenny Grohowski, the other members of KILTER, had remained throughout the whole historic event. Being on the same page in the same city at last, we got to work. What a pleasure that was—and how often can you say that about roll-up-your-sleeves creative group sessions? The pleasure wasn't in the absence of wrenching conflict—we had plenty of that. The pleasure was in everybody's willingness to consider the work itself as a living being (how ironic) coming to the worktable with its own voice. We doodled up a long scroll and turned my libretto into a sort of spatial timeline. We'd point to parts and say things like "I'm hearing this sort of thing here, but not that sort of thing…" and so on. We referred to many extant pieces of all conceivable genres as models, but only as structural or conceptual models, never as templates of how it should actually sound: the interlude-connected episodic nature of Berg's *Wozzeck*, the metamorphic modulations of Richard Strauss' *Tod und Verklärung* (*Death and Transfiguration*, a non-vocal, symphonic work), the delicate and even elegant eroticism of necrophilia in his opera *Salome*, the mutually transforming relationship between the soprano and chorus in Puccini's *La fanciulla del West*, the projection of psychology onto nature in the "Sea Interludes" of Britten's *Peter Grimes*, the inherent sarcasm in the discrete ballads found in Kurt Weill's works, and much more. Then there were Metal models (I was thinking of the structure of an Insomnium song for one choral moment, while María Elena's "My corpse, your dungeon" grew out of a response to "Your corpse, my ladder," the chorus of Jason Lekberg's "Vae Victis"), and jazz, and more. None of us knew every one of the references the others brought to the table, which was all for the better. We were moving toward a place of concord by hearing each other discuss them. Discerning what each speaker was getting at in these models was our vein of gold.

In fact, I knew and know very little about jazz, but I know that KILTER are as highly respected as musicians can be in that rarefied and I daresay somewhat haughty-to-the-point-of-exclusionary world. (Hey, I work at the

Metropolitan Opera… From haughty and exclusionary, I know.) I have always had a particular aversion to extreme progressive jazz, and specifically to the sound of the saxophone in such compositions/improvisations. When that guy (and isn't it always a guy somehow?) gets that blissed-out, spiritually superior, vaguely hallucinating look on his closed-eye face and starts blaring infernal sounds on that impossible-to-ignore instrument, I'm ten minutes late for the door. So I sought out Ed and asked him to tell me what was at stake for him in this story and in being a musician in general, and I was fascinated by what he had to say. Given this human context, I learned to listen to his music. Maybe this is what's always needed—and *all* that is needed—to connect to the music we think we'll never like (classical, Metal, *musique concrète*, prog, et al.). I don't know.

Sitting down and working, mostly with Laurent and Ed as well as a lot with Andromeda, it became clear that my distance from jazz was good for our process. It kept me in my lane. If it had been a "purely classical" (whatever that could possibly mean in this day and age, but bear with me for a moment) piece, I would have been too tempted to explain my ideas within musical metaphors that were none of my business to discuss, let alone dictate. I can hear my ego now: "For this part, may I suggest tremolo violins playing *sul ponticello* through a cello passacaglia…?" To which the only sensible response would have been a resounding "Bitch, please." Analogously, had we embarked on a pure Metal composition, I would have only been able to understand the work in terms of my Metal, which is not at all the same as the Black Metal savored by Andromeda nor the Thrash Metal (judging from his t-shirts and the posters on his studio wall) that constitute Laurent's jam. How much better it was, as it turned out, to have to express my thoughts to these musical beasts conceptually! Like, "Now for this part, I'm imagining something really big," and "This here seems like a really dissonant moment—I'm talking the full-on 'pots-and-pans' treatment," and "Well, in this interlude, they're having sex—atypical, highly unlikely sex, but sex all the same—so conjure up something to convince me of that... say, *Tristan und Isolde* meets *In the Wee Small Hours*-era Sinatra with a touch of Pantera's 'Walk.' You know, like that!" The score would come from the wide place between and connecting the boundary markers. The score, like the libretto, would come from The Border.

I felt an immediate musical connection with Laurent—not because we liked the same music, or even because we had the same understanding of how music works, but (as I had come to feel with Ed) because I sensed an allied spirit regarding the *why* of music. Talking about music with Andromeda was even easier because we drew on classical and Metal models and many others besides: she brought me up to date on some newer-than-Weill German cabaret songs that have become part of my musical library. (Note to Andromeda: to this day, whenever I find my text messages empty, I sing out the line "Kein Schwein ruft mich an!" ["No pigs call me!"—and OY does that lose something in non-musical translation!]) I never did work with Kenny Grohowski at the table, but that was fine because Kenny was the only member of KILTER I actually knew before all this began. And I knew him well, socially and musically speaking. Kenny is a nexus of music in New York—one of those people connected to so many hubs of musical creativity that his disappearance, beyond being a cause for lament in itself, could cause the entire city to collapse into the harbor. Besides being a fixture in the John Zorn world (another nexus), and his work with Imperial Triumphant and Hipster Assassins with Felix Pastorius, I knew him from his days with Resolution 15—my personal favorite local band. Who were they? Well, no easy answers there: Kenny, along with violinist Earl Maneein (another classical/metal illuminatus) and vocalist Nick Serr, somehow created the heaviest noise I had ever jumped up and down to. (And Earl and his wife, cellist Jenn DeVore, created the Metal/Hardcore/Classical string quartet SEVEN)SUNS, which became an integral part—the orchestra, in a sense—of the score of *La Suspendida*). So I trusted Kenny to do exactly what I wanted—even beyond what I even knew I wanted—in every instance. And he exceeded not only my expectations but my wildest hopes. I first heard his contributions in early performances of this piece at a notable Montreal Metal venue: the bar Foufounes Electriques. He had solo passages, but not like the drum solos I cherished as a young rock fan in the '70s. These were more like trips in the hallucinogenic sense, but with a clear sense of intention that turned suggested "pots-and-pans" passages into jaw-dropping compositions. I honestly don't know how he does it… which, of course, is why it's magical. (He's also a fellow Hispanic-with-a-*mitteleuropische*-name, so naturally I've always been inclined to dig his vibe.)

So I didn't need to work directly with Kenny on any of this. But I did work with the others, and wonderfully unpredictable things happened. When we were throwing our creative cards on the table, we each found many cases where our own "winning hands" turned out to be anything but. As Ed mentions in his essay, the phrase (I don't remember who said it; I think it was me, but like my great-grandmother's tales of the Revolution, who knows?) "It's ok to die" flew out very casually, originally referring to different options we had for the lead character. It then hung in the air until we all realized this was no mere aside but rather at the very core of why we were all here writing an opera, of all things, about a sexually actualized corpse, of all things.

This sort of epiphanic moment repeated in ways large and small throughout the creation process. I said earlier that *La Suspendida* (the title asserted itself—I never once "thought" about it) was a Tale of the Border. As such, I originally wanted—or thought I wanted—to emphasize the overt politics of the story. You know, let's smash the patriarchy while we're at it with some Brechtian agitprop. I envisioned the Gates of the City of Death as a perfectly awful border crossing station, and the Guardians of the Gate as the Bureaucrats of Eternity. (And, sorry, but could you possibly imagine a more accurate analogue of Hell?) Ed, bless his jazzy heart, flat-out rejected this vision. Fine, I thought. I will embed that within the voices of the dead, the chorus. And we did, and we liked the result much better than any of us had previously imagined we would. (I knew I would have the opportunity to express all the backstory I wanted in the "novelization" included herein: "The Vaguely Haunting and Curiously Resonant Tale of María Elena, 'La Suspendida.'" I didn't need to make KILTER conform to all my details of ideas.) Similar things happened with the casting of one soloist and chorus. I had originally imagined several soloists besides Satan's Immigration Officers: female soloists for María Elena's mother Aurora and Tanzler's possibly-imaginary ancestress The Countess (the title of María Elena's solo "The Song of the Countess" relies on the ambiguity of the word "of" and belies its origins as a featured song/showstopper by a soloist other than the star). This idea flew out the window because of logistics but also because we realized that Aurora and The Countess (and the Goddess of Love Herself) were all María Elena, or embedded within her. It was perfectly plausible to have the same character sing "The Ballad of María Elena" as well as "The Song of the Countess." Looking closer at my supposed model of Kurt Weill, I remembered that in *The Threepenny Opera*, Mack the Knife doesn't sing "The Ballad of

Mack the Knife" and Jenny didn't originally sing "Pirate Jenny." Identity in the theater, like identity in Limbo, is fluid enough to dispense with surface-level "$A = A$" ontology. I am he as you are he as you are me and we are all together.

Nor had I been able to imagine, before I heard them, the diversity of sounds that could be created by the Growlers Choir, obliviating the need for a "cast of characters" beyond the lead. They were, in real life and in sound, a cast of characters unto themselves. There was nothing I could imagine on paper that they couldn't realize in the sonic dimension. Each one of them had a back story: this one fronted a Black Metal band; that one was another conservatory-nerd-gone-bad; at least one was a budding conductor/composer; their founder/leader, Pierre-Luc Senécal, was all these things and more, someone I immediately recognized as a kindred spirit and an ally in much more than musical taste. That night at Foufounes, when I saw Pierre-Luc conducting the music while standing directly next to a mosh pit that erupted spontaneously, I had that strange and satisfying feeling of completeness I imagine sci-fi heroes feel directly before being beamed back up to the mothership.

As with details, so with the piece as a whole…. We didn't know this opera would become about acceptance and harmony with eternity. It just asserted this conclusion on us as it unfolded. We became aware of the epoch, so to speak, of the action as that nano-moment between life and death which both science and mythology concur exists, however briefly, for everyone—but looking at it from some point of view that makes it a very long moment (twenty years in historical time, about an hour in opera time). We all felt a connection to this suspended moment, each for various reasons. I was dealing with some health issues throughout the composition process. In fact, the very night we did our first live performance of the almost-complete work (January 12th, 2023, at the wonderful Culture Lab LIC in Queens) my body gave me some distinct and unmistakable indicators that the bladder cancer tumors which had been removed the previous month were back and spreading fast. Yup, that very night. I called the doctor and arranged for tests that would either say "false alarm, all clear" or "you're going to die and there is nothing to be done about it." As it turned out, I was neither—or rather, both. I was neither cured nor in immediate danger of death, but the possibility of metastasis remained and so the future possibility of a terminal diagnosis could not be entirely eliminated. Of course, it never can be, ever, for anyone. But that night, the fork in the road seemed stark and ominous. There I was—a large, wordy version of Schrödinger's Cat as Librettist—and I spent some time railing at God and at Time, asking how the HELL I could be expected to walk around and act all cool and shit when I didn't know if I was going to be dead in a few months or not? I quickly realized I had been living in this "in-between" space since my first malignant diagnosis 18 years previously, and everyone I knew who had any cancer or HIV or really any number of diagnoses was also living there, and basically this is how everyone lives, all the time, whether they know it or not. That "moment" between life and death is extended far beyond the brief instant we imagine it to be. It's a state of existence unto itself, and worthy of respectful consideration, almost as much as the states of Life and Death which cannot be discerned without it. That Border between Life and Death is not "nothing at all." Rather, "Fuck you, it's everything." It is the place that made the opera *La Suspendida* possible to create and offer to you.

THE OPERA

LA SUSPENDIDA

SYNOPSIS
of the Opera *La Suspendida*

María Elena, a beautiful 21-year-old divorcee from Cuba, dies of tuberculosis in Key West. As the sun rises along the Atlantic coast, Shades of the realm of Death call forth the souls of all who died overnight in The Americas to enter the eternal Gates. María Elena thanks them for the invitation but prefers to remain outside the Gates, suspended between realms of Life and Death. They insist she enter, but she utilizes fresh infusions of seed from Tanzler, the doctor who treated her, to remain where she is: Tanzler's sexual obsession with her didn't die when she did, and now his acts of necrophilia empower her to claim her own realm. In her arguments with the Dead, she explains to them that Tanzler once had a dream-visitation from his grandmother, a Countess who died before he was born: she promised to create an ideal woman for him. When he met María Elena years later, he instantly recognized her as the Promised Ideal. As he loved her before she was born, now he loves her after she's died. Unseen, he infuses María Elena once again with seed, to the indignant disgust of the Shades. Their arrogance triggers her rage, and she makes them watch her dominate Tanzler into sexual service. The encounter proves too much for Tanzler, who dies as he climaxes.

María Elena is deflated to hear his name called in the next roll call of the newly dead, knowing she has lost her powers. The Dead console her: there is no shame in joining them now that she has had her moment of complete self-determination. She moves toward the Gates, accepting death like everyone else.

La Suspendida

An Opera in Jazz and Metal for Female Soloist and Chorus

Libretto by William Berger

I
Overture: Death & Transfiguration

*

II
Limbo: A Place with No Weather (Solo, María Elena)

> I don't hate this place
> It's not Cuba, or Florida
> Not hot, not cold
> No weather at all
> In my body, yet free from it
>
> I never loved my body much
> It always felt like someone else
> It's starting to feel right at last

Right here, right now, at last

Adios old world, old ways
Marriage, home, family
I sense a new love here. Now
Outside of time
Unlike any love there's ever been

I revel in the pleasure
And let go of the pain
In this new land, that is no land
This place between realms
This place with no weather

*

III
Interlude: Arrival

Come from afar,
Foreign lover,
Though I be unalive
Cross the great line,
Drench me,
That I be not all dead

*

IV
Laudes Mortuorum & Roll Call of the Newly Dead (Chorus)

Morning comes.
shhh
Morning comes to the eastern shore.
shhh
Reveal the shadows gathered there.
The newly dead of the Americas await
our summons across the sand.
Arise.
Arise, Shades.
Arise, Shades.
Fall in the parade as single tears.
Augment the ocean of perpetual death.
Arise, Shades.
You must obey.
We know not of light or time.
You who still do must pass through.
Come! Come, we will teach you
the timeless ways of this land.
Come shed your name, your clock, your pain.
Come shed your name, your clock, your pain.

Kiko da Silva, Rio de Janeiro, 17, knife wound.
Hattie May Johnson, Norfolk, 89, loneliness.

Ryan O'Malley, New York, 46, heart attack.
Kwe'Tshito of Kanawahkee, 52, frozen.

Come shed your name, your clock, your pain.
Come shed your name, your clock, your pain.

Maria Elena Milagros, Key West, 21, tuberculosis...

Maria Elena Milagros, Key West, 21, tuberculosis.

ALL SHADES MUST COMPLY!!!!

*

V
A Decision

*

VI
The Ballad of María Elena (Solo, María Elena)

Thank you so much… I hate to be rude
Not choosing one or the other
But I have the means to choose something new
I even got help from my mother

As for me...
I won't listen to your rule book
As for me,
I'll just stay here in this place eternally
Eternally

Cuba was my home but I chose to roam
My husband decided to leave me;
Our child was born dead I sought out instead,
a homeland that would not deceive me
As for me,
I don't stay where I don't want to
You can see

I went to Key West
Doctor Tanzler was obsessed
Obsessed with me, living, dying then lifeless
He did me then,
He does me now
And I'm kind of liking it like this

As for me,
I've created quite a system
I can be
In control in life and death and in-between
I like it here,
The in-between tier
In this limbo locale with no weather
Tanzlers's living lust,

In this cunt of dust,
Means I can stay here forever

As for me
I've got myself a husband
Who loves me as I am
As I am, not how he thinks I should be

Mama does my hair and make-up up there
Then he fucks the corpse that he attended
I vibe with his vibe I gladly imbibe
The essence that keeps me suspended
As for me
I don't need to join your chorus
As for me
I can live here in control eternally

I know it's odd
I know we're not a typical pair
Quirky and young
His perv intentions cross cosmic dimensions
No other man is so well hung
As for me
I'm not merely in a coma
I'm alive!!
After dying way too young I plan to thrive!

*

VII
Arguments at the Gates of Death, Part 1:
You can't drag me through your gate (Tutti)

Chorus:
They don't exist,
Venus, Ishtar
There are no Goddesses of Power…
Only human fear of us,
the dead.

María Elena:
You say he loves my corpse
Because he fears death,
but I don't care
I know that nothing can bring me back to life
But as long as I get his fresh seed,
You can't drag me through your gate

*

VIII
Interlude: Innocence

Come from afar,
Foreign lover,
Though I be unalive

Cross the great line,
Drench me,
That I be not all dead

*

IX
Arguments at the Gates of Death, Part 2: You don't remember what flesh is (Tutti)

Chorus:
If Love is a god, then so is Time
A god with the power to bring all here

María Elena:
You don't know shit if you believe
That Time's a stronger god than Love.
How many lovers have loved beyond death?
Didn't Thelma and Louise love into the abyss?
Didn't Tristan and Isolde grow trees
That intertwined above their graves?

Chorus:
They died together
They were equal
Their love did not inhabit separate worlds

María Elena:
But others did. And you allowed it!
Victoria shaved Albert's statue everyday
Shah Jahan's dead wife lies in
the world's finest monument!
People travel far and wide to
behold how much he loved her.
Pornography in marble!

Chorus:
They loved with souls, not flesh
Much less did they mingle flesh and dust

María Elena:
You don't remember what flesh is
Flesh is pure, even when decayed
It's only the soul that sins
You don't remember what flesh is!

Chorus:
It cannot be
It will not pass
The tests of science and morals

*

X
Song of the Countess (Solo, María Elena)

María Elena:
I tell you it is, and if you must know,
Why don't you ask the old Countess,
Back there behind your gates?
Or can't you find her?
Can't you tell one from another?

Chorus:
At night, all cats are gray

María Elena:
Well I can tell her story myself,
Tanzler told me enough times
He said she was his grandmother,
But I doubt it
All men think they're noble

The Goddess of Love is a fraud and a bitch
Ruling the world as a whore divine
With a thousand faces and a name for each
And I am her slave, as you, Sir, are mine
She's Venus, Ishtar, Freia, Rati
But worse than you know—she's also a thief
She makes people want what's not theirs to take
And lust for those things that only bring grief:
Caligula fucked his old granny

And Xerxes fell in lust with a tree
Pasiphaë chose a bull as a stud,
To name but the worst from antiquity.
All may refuse and reject her decree
Yet all are controlled by her sway;
They may well object or they might agree
All that results is that all will obey.

Now I bring you a gift from the Goddess,
Something that's never before even been.
Won't you be pleased to be forced to commit
An awesomely twisted original sin?

We're sending to you a passion unique
A lust more perverse than a bull or a tree…
You'll love a woman who doesn't exist
Yet owned by a mistress who's yet to be.

We've probed your most secret dreams
And according to these we'll craft her
And her flesh will be yours to love
Forever and ever, then evermore after

Now I bring you a gift from the Goddess
Something that's never before even been.
Won't you be pleased to be forced to commit
An awesomely twisted original sin?
And her flesh will be yours to love
Forever and ever, then evermore after….

*

XI
Interlude: Moments of Stillness

*

XII
Arguments at the Gates of Death, Part 3:
The hypocrites of the light (Tutti)

Chorus:
If sex and love are one
Then your man sins twice
Against the God of Time:
he fucked you
both before birth and after death
he fucked you

María Elena:
Didn't my first husband do the same?
He left me when I bore a corpse.
Our stillborn child was the death of his future,
His failure, his first death of many

Chorus:
A sin against nature
A sin against time
A sin against love

María Elena:

Everyone does this…
Don't you see?
Every time they buy stock,
or plant a tree
It's fucking the future
To dodge Death's decree.
In the dimension of Love,
Time has no sway.
Either it's love,
or it just fades away

Chorus:
Fucking a corpse is a sin

María Elena:
Everyone fucks the dead,
You self-righteous prigs

Chorus:
Fucking a corpse is a sin

María Elena:
Everyone fucks the dead,
You self-righteous prigs,
No better than us
And far less forthright.

Chorus:
Your sin is greater

María Elena:
Tell me again
How much you all love
Princess Diana,
poor Marilyn Monroe
La Divina Callas –
Can you let them rest, at last?

Chorus:
Your sin is greater
You upend all that is.
Your sin is greater

María Elena:
And isn't that Lenin I see
Over there, in this limbo

Chorus:
You are desperate

María Elena:
He is not buried yet
Suspended
Adored by his few
Remaining devotees

Chorus:
You are merely desperate

María Elena:

And let's not even talk
About Christ, you freaks…
Whom you never let rest
As you get on your knees
And beg Him to return

Chorus:
You are desperately
clinging to life
By a phallic thread

Let go

María Elena:
It's only a sin now
Because a woman calls the shot

Chorus:
Let go

María Elena:
That's when the living speak
Of sin and perversion
And crimes against Nature.
I see the dead
Are no better than
The hypocrites of the Light.
I'll show you my power
I'll make you watch
So you have to admit

Your hypocrisy
Your hatred inspires me
To new heights of love.
I've never felt stronger
Or sexier then now
I declare
I declare
I declare my body
My own,
And this body
Will be obeyed!

*

XIII
My Corpse, Your Dungeon (Solo, María Elena)

Chorus:
{sounds of revulsion}
Vile! Vile! Vile!

María Elena:
My corpse, your dungeon… Right?
You love me, tho I'm dead inside
I'll let you, tho you haven't died
My corpse, your dungeon… Right?
I triumphed, the first time I died

I'd die twice if you were not inside

Chorus:
It reeks of life
It reeks of life

María Elena:
Obey me, my thrall
And love me once more
But way more than before
I'll embrace my power
And make the dead watch it all
A show of compliance…
Hold my pale fragile sheath
Above you… Crawl beneath,
Surrender your manhood
To my act of defiance
Thus I command, my Drone,
Do what you're good for
But harder and more,
So I can reign solely
In this realm of my own.

My corpse, your dungeon… Right?
You love me, tho I'm dead inside

Chorus:
Sin against nature and Time

María Elena:

I'll let you, tho you haven't died
My corpse, your dungeon… Right?
I triumphed, the first time I died

Chorus:
You cling to life!
María Elena:
I'd die twice if you were not inside

Chorus:
You must let go

María Elena:
Water my dust bowl
With your devoted seed
The one thing I need,
More than ever before,
In my cold alpha hole
Confess what you crave!
Let all the dead see.
You're nothing without me,
Unsung and forgotten,
Except as my slave
Now give it all here,
Fuck with your whole life,
Your dominant wife
Now needs to blast off
To the next stratosphere

My corpse, your dungeon… Right?
You love me, tho I'm dead inside
I'll let you, tho you haven't died
My corpse, your dungeon… Right?
I triumphed, the first time I died
I'd die twice if you weren't inside

*

XIV
Interlude: Climax

*

XV
Afterglow (Solo, María Elena)

Where am I now?
I got here… how?
Seems like the same spot…
But, then again, not
I haven't moved…
But everything feels
Transfixed,
Transformed
Changed

*

XVI
Double Call: Laudes Mortuarum Reprise and Finale (tutti)

Maria Elena:
Why? Why? Why? Why?
Why must I hear, why must I hear,
Must I hear them, I hear them still!
I wish I had music
To drown out their sound.

Chorus :
Morning comes
Shhh
Morning comes to the Eastern Shore
Shhh
Reveal the shadows gathered there,
The newly dead of the Americas,
Await our summons across the sand

Maria Elena:
Why can't I block them out?

Chorus :
Arise, Arise, Shades!
Arise, Shades!
Fall in the parade,
As single tears

Augment the ocean
of perpetual death

María Elena:
I wish I could fuck
Louder than last time
And not have to hear
The choir of the dead.

Chorus :
Arise, Shades! Arise

Suzy Kowolski, 56, Asbury Park… Car crash

María Elena:
Their song wears me out!
Tanzler, come back…

Chorus:
Elgin McKay, 24, Kingston… gunshot

María Elena:
Tanzler, come back…
Come serve me again
As big as last time.

Chorus :
Raúl Rossi, 47, La Plata… cancer

María Elena:
Fill my dark, dank womb

With your seed of light,

Chorus:
Catalina Pérez, 16, Veracruz… Died in childbirth

María Elena:
Keep me suspended
Between two worlds

Chorus:
Carl Tanzler, 75, Key West…

María Elena:
Dead? Dead?
Tanzler is dead?

He can't help me now.
Is there another
Who'd answer the call
To a body like this?

All men are quitters,
All men are shadows,
All men make chaos,
Then vanish below
All men leave me,
All men deceive me,
No man is sure,
No man is my cure,
They couldn't save me there,

And they won't save me here.

Chorus:
Come, Tanzler,
also called Doctor,
and Count von Tanzler;
Cause of death: Heart attack during sex… with a corpse

María Elena:
Fucking a corpse!
A cause of death
That's a final joke
The ultimate lay,
His final day
Sex so intense
It's a capital offense

But how can I stay here
If he's no longer up there?
I don't want to die yet,
And be part of a crowd…
The dreary masses
Of dull gray shades.
I died once already
Too soon: never again!
Let no borders hold me!
I fly above them.
I am the unique one,
Created by magic,

To exist before birth
And persist after death.
I am La Suspendida,
The genre of One!

Chorus:
María Elena Milagros, Key West, 21, tuberculosis

María Elena:
My name… again…

Chorus:
María Elena Milagros, Key West, 21, tuberculosis

María Elena:
No more Tanzler

Chorus:
No more necro

María Elena:
No more Body

Chorus:
No more sickness

María Elena:
No more living

Chorus:

No more prayers

María Elena:
No more loving

Chorus:
No more memories

María Elena:
No more messages
From the living world
Nothing left
To pretend I'm alive
Nothing more
To keep me afloat

Chorus:
Daughter, daughter, daughter
Come home

María Elena:
I thought I cheated life and death
And found my own space
Between kingdoms
Where I alone ruled
But that was a dream.

I didn't want to need him,
To whore my corpse…
I only wanted to take control

Of my own life,
Of my own body,
My own fate.
When I dared to rise over him
From my position below,
Was that moment "love"?

*

XVII
Lullabye (Tutti)

Chorus:
Come, come
It's ok to expire
Come, come
Once your goal is won
Come, come
You can join the choir
Come, come
Once your solo's done

María Elena:
Mother, true mother
Not countess, nor she
Who once gave me birth
But all cradle Earth,
I've craved you so long

> But I didn't know how to come home
> As victor, not victim,
> Let me lie among you
> Let me rest at last
> I've craved you so long
> But now I know how to come home
> Yes, yes, yes

*

(Fin. The End. Das fucking Ende).

ABOUT THE COLLABORATORS OF

LA SUSPENDIDA

ANDROMEDA ANARCHIA
Auto-Bio

My name is ANDROMEDA ANARCHIA and I am a New York-based singer, composer, lyricist and producer from Switzerland. I started out as a classically trained soprano (Konservatorium Winterthur in Switzerland with Tenor Paul Steiner; advanced training with Mezzo-Soprano Margo Weiskam from Berlin, Germany) but did not want to become a traditional opera singer. Therefore, I switched to contemporary singing, first to jazz (Jazzschule Zurich with Renata Friederich, and additional training with Efrat Alony at Jazzschule Bern), then to heavy metal and extreme metal (Training with Mark B. Lay, Soren Sedit and Mateusz Sibilia) and even to cabaret music. However, I also immersed myself in the world of freely improvised and experimental music, specializing along the way in the eclectic world of progressive, experimental and avant-garde metal music—musical styles I've loved since childhood. Since the age of five, I have always written my own music, mostly in the form of songs, but also compositions for instrumental music. I love to use my voice as a versatile instrument, combining different vocal styles in all possible and (almost) impossible ways: classical singing, contemporary singing as well as extended vocal techniques such as metal screams. Nowadays I perform mainly in the context of avant-garde/progressive/extreme/experimental metal and metal jazz. At this moment, I am known as the lead singer and frontwoman of the internationally acclaimed operatic black metal band FOLTERKAMMER and as the producer of the prog rock/art song project *DARK MATTERS*. It's a great honor to be a regular collaborator for metal-jazz trio KILTER (*La Suspendida* /*Axiom*) and for the avant-garde black metal band IMPERIAL TRIUMPHANT. The debut EP of my project *DARK MATTERS* was nominated for the Independent Music Award (NYC, 2019) and I was listed as "Best Extreme Vocalist 2020" by *RETUMBA* Magazine (Mexico).

Collaborations and guest appearances since 2018:

- IMPERIAL TRIUMPHANT (NYC, USA): *Spirit of Ecstasy* (2022), *Alphaville* (2020), *Vile Luxury* (2018)
- KILTER (Metal-Jazz— NYC, USA): *La Suspendida* (2022/23), *Axiom* (2020)
- Laurent David's *NAKED* (jazz—Paris, France)
- MOTIONFIX (experimental hip hop—Seattle USA: Heart Hooks)
- Panos Megarchiotis (Classical Music/Bossa Nova—Switzerland and Greece)
- Von Pourquery (Alternative Pop—Paris, France: Starlight).

*

KILTER

Band Bio

KILTER is a New York based, award-winning AVANT METAL-JAZZ trio, existing since Summer 2018. Created and produced by the French bassist Laurent David, the band includes Kenny Grohowski on drums and Ed RosenBerg III on saxophones. After the release of their Debut-EP, in December 2018, for which they received the Independent Music Award 2020 (in Jazz EP category), trio KILTER released *AXIOM* in February 2020 and *SYS* (2021)—dark and powerful music inspired by the unrelenting hustle and grind of New York City. All KILTER musicians are internationally recognized and touring worldwide: Laurent David is known from SHIJIN, The Way Things Go, Guillaume Perret's Electric Epic, Ibrahim Maalouf, Yael Naim; Ed RosenBerg III is known for bands like Jerseyband and Heart Of Barf, and holds a PhD in composition; Kenny Grohowski works regularly for John Zorn, Secret Chiefs 3, Imperial Triumphant, Felix Pastorius & The Hipster Assassins, et al.

ALBUMS AND PRODUCTIONS:

- *LA SUSPENDIDA* metal jazz opera (work in progress, 2022-2024)

- *SYS* (2021)

- *AXIOM* (2020) • *EP* (2019)

*

GROWLERS CHOIR
Bio

The first growlers choir in history. Composed solely of metal vocalists called "growlers," Growlers Choir blends Metal and experimental music in a way that is unique and groundbreaking. Hailing from Montreal, Canada, one of the world's capitals of Metal music, the 13 metal vocalists ensemble was dreamt up by composer Pierre-Luc Senécal in 2016. What may have been a wild fantasy for many Metalheads was finally brought to fruition in May 2019, when the band took the stage for their first public performance. Their first piece, the mythical "The Dayking," triggered a frenzy of ecstatic comments, calling it "masterfully arranged," "mindblowing," "a ritual of summoning demons from the other dimensions," a descent "into literal unbridled chaos." This success was in no small part due to the lead speaker of the piece, Fortner Anderson. Pioneer of the spoken word scene in Montreal, his reading of his text "The Dayking" has been described as dramatically poignant, visceral and riveting. Growlers Choir has since dedicated itself to producing ambitious concerts, creating bewitching music and exploring vocal techniques. Fascinated by Extreme Metal as well as a variety of throat singing techniques, Growlers Choir showcases the sonic potential of the voice and demonstrates its extraordinary properties, both sensual and monstrous. In May 2021, Growlers Choir headlined the Festival international de musique actuelle de Victoriaville, one of the most respected events of its kind in North America. In June 2021, it collaborated with classical choir Temps Fort for the concert "Extreme Vocals." The event comprised 60 minutes of music for double choir (14 growlers and 24 singers) in a 50,000 square feet church. Growlers Choir's original musical hydra has attracted a variety of public and media such as *Vice News*, the popular Quebecer talk show *Tout le monde en parle* and *MetalSucks*, one of the most important media of the Metal music scene. Growlers Choir is a grant recipient from the Canadian Council of the Arts, the Conseil des arts et des lettres du Québec, and the Conseil des arts de Montréal.

SEVEN)SUNS
Quartet Bio

SEVEN)SUNS is a string quartet that plays dystopian music rooted in the language of avant-Metal and Hardcore. Their repertoire is drawn from works by members of the group, re-imagined string quartet versions of Metal and Hardcore songs, as well as music from the Western art music tradition. SEVEN)SUNS has played diverse venues such as New York's Terminal 5, The Gallery at Le Poisson Rouge, Saint Vitus Bar, The Cell Theater, Firehouse Space, Shapeshifter Lab, and The Knitting Factory. In addition to sharing the bill and touring with such Metal bands such as Candiria, Cellar Darling, Car Bomb, Empire Shall Fall, and Cleric, SEVEN)SUNS has been presented by the Tribeca New Music Festival regularly over the years and has twice been awarded a residency at the prestigious Avaloch Farm Music Institute. SEVEN)SUNS did a cover Pantera's "This Love/Domination" and a cover of The Dillinger Escape

Plan's "43% Burnt." The videos received over 100,000 views combined and led to features on numerous heavy metal websites such as Metal Injection, SkullsandBones.com, and MetalSucks.net, among others. This led to a collaboration with The Dillinger Escape Plan. SEVEN)SUNS is prominently featured on their final album *Dissociation* (2016), and performed with them on their now-legendary final show in New York in 2017. SEVEN)SUNS received a generous grant from the Brooklyn Arts Council to write and perform a piece titled "Songs of the Voiceless" based on visits to Rikers Island Correctional Facility in New York City. The quartet members volunteered there, playing music for inmates in conjunction with the Rangjung Dharma Prison Project, a Tibetan Buddhist organization whose mission is to teach meditation and provide guidance to inmates. The pieces resulting from that experience, among others, appeared on their debut album, *For The Hearts Still Beating*, released in 2017 on Party Smasher Inc. SEVEN)SUNS is featured on new albums by Thought Crimes, Imperial Triumphant, So Hideous, and Amanda Palmer.

ABOUT THE LIBRETTIST/AUTHOR

William Berger is an American author, radio host and commentator (The Metropolitan Opera, NYC), and lecturer. Born in Los Angeles in 1961, he grew up in a bilingual (Spanish and English) and multicultural (Mexican, Italian, and Jewish) home. After spending some teen years in various places in the US and Europe, he studied Latin and Italian Literature at UC Santa Cruz. He worked during this time at the San Francisco Opera in various capacities, including merchandising and translating for the Artists' Liaison. Moving to New York in 1984, he worked in architecture/design, and was a part-time instructor of Italian and Romance Languages at Baruch College. He has written on a variety of subjects as a free-lance writer, including architecture, religion, and sports. He is the author of several books on opera. His more recent books include *Speaking of Wagner: Talking to Audiences About* The Ring Of The Nibelung, *Seeking the Sublime Cache,* and *The Metaliad*, a full-length mock-epic poem in the style of Ariosto and Byron dealing with New York's Metal community and the fight against neo-fascists. He is a frequent lecturer/speaker at a variety of venues, including The Embassy of Finland, The Italian Cultural Institute (NY), the Smithsonian Institute, The Wagner Society of America (in New York, San Francisco, L.A., Washington DC, Chicago, Dallas, and Boston), the National Museum of Women in the Arts (DC), The Fountain Theatre (L.A.), Berklee College of Music (Boston), The Canadian Museum of Human Rights (Winnipeg), Society of the Four Arts (Palm Beach), and writes for a wide range of institutions, including the opera companies of Seattle, San Francisco, Houston, Maine, Philadelphia, Austin, Los Angeles, and Washington DC, as well as the Liceu of Barcelona and Paris' Théâtre aux Champs-Élysées. He was the host of WNYC's "Overnight Music" in 2004-2006, which included the weekly show "El Salón," focusing on Hispanic issues in classical music. He has been a writer, producer, and on-air commentator for the Metropolitan Opera since 2006, appears on the Met's *Live in HD* telecast series, is heard on the podcast series "In Focus," and is also responsible for the Met's Opera

Quiz. Berger is a keen and active supporter of new music in a variety of genres, especially his predominant passion of Metal. He frequently produces music, spoken word, and performing arts showcases combining established and emerging talent. He lives in New York City's East Village with his husband Stephen J. Miller since (*de facto*) 1996 and (*de jure*) 2013.

*

Also by William Berger

Wagner Without Fear (Vintage Books, 1998)

Verdi With a Vengeance (Vintage Books, 2000)

"Chris DeBlasio" in *Loss Within Loss: Artists in the Age of AIDS*, edited by Edmund White (University of Wisconsin Press, 2001)

The NPR Curious Listener's Guide to the Opera (Penguin Putnam, 2002)

Puccini Without Excuses (Vintage Books, 2005)

Speaking of Wagner: Talking to Audiences about The Ring of the Nibelung (Academica Press, 2020)

Seeking the Sublime Cache: Opera Articles Selected and Written by William Berger, with a Foreword by Jamie Barton (The Prime Convergence, 2021)

The Metaliad: an Epic of Heavy Brooklyn (in Ottava Rima) (The Prime Convergence, 2022)

Archived Webinars:

The Story of Opera (8 episodes)

Opera and Film (8 episodes)

Opera and Metal (1 episode)

Video:

Rodríguez furioso: a live Ensemble Reading from The Metaliad *(10/23/2022)*

For more information, see WilliamBergerPresents.com

Made in the USA
Middletown, DE
11 June 2024